the essential eye

BRITISH AIRWAYS
London eye

conceived and designed by
marks barfield architects

British Airways London Eye is an attraction
managed by The Tussaud's Group

Written by Kester Rattenbury

the essential eye
foreword

Dear Friend

Thank you for visiting the British Airways London Eye, also previously known as the Millennium Wheel.

From the moment the giant steel rim of the wheel was successfully lifted off its temporary islands in the River Thames, we knew that an incredible challenge had been won and that the London skyline had fundamentally changed. It was, in fact, the second time we had attempted the lift – our first attempt, just one month earlier, had ended in embarrassing failure with the eyes of the world's media there to witness and report it. But the press and public reactions were fantastic. We were inundated with letters of support and encouragement. People seemed to appreciate – and wanted to understand – the difficulties involved in raising the largest object ever lifted from the horizontal to the vertical. The engineering team behind the lift was magnificent. No recriminations, no despair, just a deep determination to fix the problem and make it work. We can't tell you how much respect we have for their ingenuity, integrity and straightforward loyalty.

Six years earlier, the London Eye had begun life on our kitchen table as an entry to an open ideas competition to design a millennium landmark. We didn't win the competition – in fact there were no winners – but the idea was born to provide a publicly accessible vantage point from which to appreciate one of the best cityscapes in the world. We pursued our dream, creating the company to develop the idea, negotiating our way through the legal and planning

complexities of the project, and looked for partners to help us make it a reality. It was the *Evening Standard* that first gave our design the oxygen of publicity, bringing it to the attention of British Airways who shared the vision, became our partners and provided the necessary loans to get the project off the ground.

As the project developed, everyone was inspired with one objective in mind – to create a new perspective on London and an exciting new way to see and understand one of the greatest cities on earth. Of course, designing and building the largest observation wheel in the world was always going to be an incredible technical challenge, and it was an immense privilege to collaborate with some of the most distinguished and talented engineers we have ever had the pleasure of working with. From the beginning, we wanted to create something uplifting, something that would delight, that would be light and airy, and that would be delicate on the London skyline – a symbol looking to the future.

We are incredibly proud of the team that, against the odds, has brought you the London Eye as well as the fantastic team that operates it for you today, and we owe a huge debt of gratitude to everyone who lent us their support and helped to make it happen. It has been the most amazing experience for us all, for everyone involved. We hope it is an amazing experience for you too.

David Marks and Julia Barfield

contents

design & construction

eye view

design & construction
the concept

The British Airways London Eye is one of the most spectacular and popular attractions in Europe, drawing visitors from far and wide. Its success is unquestionable, as is its popularity with tourists and Londoners alike. Yet it was conceived and designed by a husband and wife team, in minimal time and against considerable odds. In fact, of all the records the London Eye has broken, perhaps the most astounding fact is that it was ever built at all.

Designed by David Marks and Julia Barfield, the drawings for the London Eye were originally submitted for a competition, run by the *Sunday Times* newspaper and The Architecture Foundation. The idea was to find a suitable project that would help to mark the dawning of the new millennium in the city. Ironically, all of the submitted entries were rejected and the competition was eventually abandoned.

Yet Marks Barfield Architects knew they had a project worth pursuing. Their plan – for the biggest observation wheel in the world – would celebrate Britain's technological innovation and provide a spectacular panorama of London. Like the Eiffel Tower in Paris, which was originally built as a temporary structure for the city's Great Exhibition in 1889, the London Eye would animate the skyline and provide a new perspective on the city. David and Julia decided to continue with the project and formed a company to develop the idea, backing it with their own money. London's daily paper the *Evening Standard* picked up the story, helping to champion the cause. Then British Airways got on board and a partnership was formed...

'The ingredients of the wheel are simple – a universal desire to see the earth and cities from a great height, and the natural human fascination with scale, daring structure, and beauty.'

Julia Barfield, Marks Barfield Architects

LEFT A scale model of the Eye and London was built, in order to gauge the structure's size and impact in relation to the rest of the city. The model was a key element in acquiring planning permission and is still kept on show at the Marks Barfield offices.

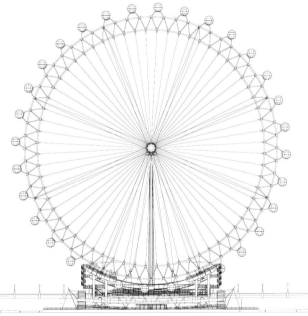

ABOVE Marks Barfield's design for the largest observation wheel in the world was originally bigger, containing 60 capsules instead of the final count of 32 shown here. Unlike the traditional Ferris wheel, designed by George Ferris, the capsules are fixed outside the rim and rotate mechanically.

design & construction
the challenge

The British Airways London Eye breaks many records in terms of size, technology and design. At 135 metres tall, it is the largest observation wheel in the world – and is also one of the highest structures in London. It is the only cantilevered structure of its kind in the world and is, interestingly, the only one ever built over water. Moreover, the Eye was constructed flat on the river and hoisted up into the vertical position in one operation. It is the largest structure ever raised in this manner – and the most dramatic piece of construction ever seen in the capital.

Yet the London Eye, which can hold up to 800 people at any one time, is also a temporary structure – the original planning permission lasts only for five years. Unlike the Eiffel Tower, which was constructed using over 2 million hot driven rivets, the wheel was designed and built so that it could be dismantled and moved to a different location if necessary.

The work and planning required by the team in order to put the project together was immense. Built in less than 16 months, the London Eye is a truly international structure, involving the teamwork of various European engineers. Specialist firms and designers had to invent almost every component and construction technique, as well as organise transportation to get the Eye up the River Thames to its chosen location. Everything was specially fabricated, tested, refined and tested again. And all of this had to be done to a deadline of New Year's Eve, 1999.

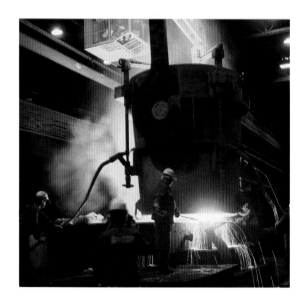

An international structure, the London Eye employed the help of British, French, Dutch, Italian and Czech workers.

More than 1,700 people worked on the London Eye project – and that's in addition to an entire alpine village that turned out to test the embarkation procedures for the capsules. Marks Barfield Architects led the design team from the UK, with their engineers and project management firm, but various parts were built in other European countries.

The wheel was developed and produced by steelwork contractors based in the Netherlands. The cast steel elements – the spindle and the hinges – were made in the Czech Republic. The steel cables, which tie the structure together, were specially spun in Italy. And the capsules, which were co-designed by Marks Barfield and an architect/boat designer in Devon, were developed and built by cable-car specialists in the French Alps. The glass for the capsules is double-curved and laminated – something that had never been achieved before – and was specially made in a workshop just outside Venice. After all this, every component was separately checked by a firm of independent engineers.

FAR LEFT Construction workers pour the molten steel into a special mould, in order to form the two huge feet that support the A-frame legs. This work was carried out at the Skoda steel factory in the Czech Republic, where the process is still monitored and controlled by hand.

LEFT An engineer carefully fits the hub over the spindle, at the Hollandia factory located in the Netherlands. This photograph illustrates the sheer size of the components.

BELOW One of the largest floating cranes in Europe was required to lift the hub and spindle assembly onto the temporary platform built over the River Thames. The single heaviest piece to be raised in this way, the component collectively weighs around 335 tonnes – almost the equivalent of a Boeing 747 aeroplane.

design & construction
the components

The frame of the London Eye is a huge latticed 'bicycle wheel' structure, with a diameter of 135m and weighing some 1,500 tonnes. The central hub rotates on a spindle that is 25m long, and is fixed to the rim with two sets of cables; one holding the rim in place, the other ensuring the hub and rim move together as the wheel turns.

Shipping these components up the river brought its own set of complications. Delivery had to be carefully timed to co-ordinate with the tides, so that the large parts could be safely negotiated under London's bridges. Southwark Bridge was the tightest squeeze – with clearance reaching as little as 40 centimetres. One of the world's tallest floating cranes was used to lift the massive quarter sections of the rim onto the eight temporary platforms, where they were welded together.

The central spindle of the wheel and the hub (two cast steel rings 4.5 metres in diameter) were held in position on a central platform as the cables were fixed. The radial cables are only 70mm thick and made up of 121 individual strands in six layers. (To this scale, a bicycle wheel's spokes would be only ⅛mm thick.) They were laid out on a barge, fixed in position and tightened.

The great A-frame legs – 58 metres long and straddling 20 metres – are supported by massive foundations and are tied back by further cables anchored below Jubilee Gardens.

RIGHT AND FAR RIGHT A ladder runs up the centre of one of the A-frame legs, providing access for general maintenance. Taut cables, anchored in the ground beneath Jubilee Gardens, keep the A-frame in position.

design & construction
the capsules

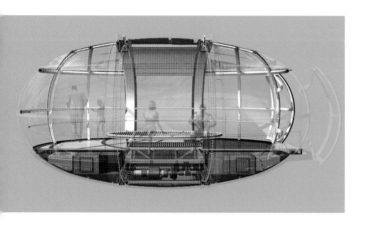

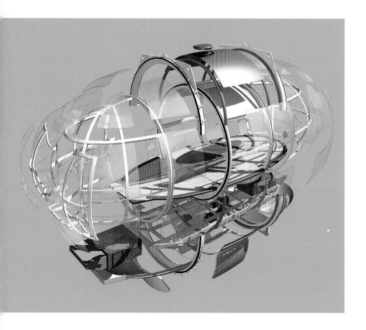

The passenger capsules of the London Eye incorporate an entirely new design form for observation wheels. Ordinarily, 'gondolas' are suspended from the rim, keeping upright through gravity (as with the original Ferris design). However, for the first time in wheel construction, the Eye's capsules are not suspended. Rather, they are fixed to the outside of the main frame, giving a unique and spectacular 360-degree panorama at the top.

Every part of the capsules had to be specially designed. Each of the egg-shaped pods is held by two huge ring-bearings, within which the capsules are driven mechanically. The French cable-car firm, who worked with Marks Barfield and architect/boat designer Nic Bailey, built a test rig that was used to simulate the effects of turning and passenger movement. The aim was to minimise the potential for uncomfortable swaying if everyone inside moved at the same time.

The pen-end shape of the steel framework, with its tight curves and precise shape, was particularly difficult to manufacture. Similarly, the double-curved glass needed to be stronger and have greater curvature than ever achieved before – the Italian manufacturers

TOP LEFT A computer-generated illustration reveals a long section of the capsule. The stability system and air conditioning can be seen below the floor.

BOTTOM LEFT An exploded view of a capsule illustrates the positioning of all 36 different glass panels required for each pod. All of the glass panels are double-curved.

'We tried all kinds of specialist designers and manufacturers – for tube trains, taxis, monorail…'

David Marks, Marks Barfield Architects

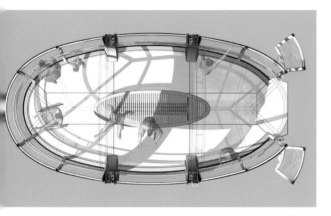

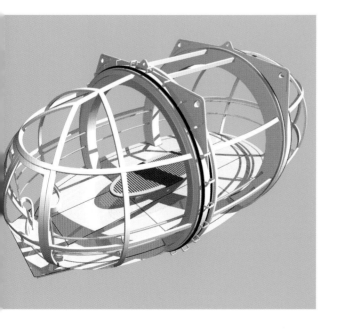

TOP LEFT A computer-generated illustration shows a plan view of the capsule interior with open doors.

BOTTOM LEFT This illustration shows the structural frame and mounting rings on each capsule. Four fixing points, for use on the rim support frame, can be seen at the top of the capsule.

BELOW The capsules were designed to a maximum width of 4 metres, in order to enable their unescorted transportation along French roads. The 'convoi exceptionnel' became a familiar sight to villagers throughout the autumn of 1999 as the capsules were transported to the coast, ready for shipping to Britain.

design & construction
the capsules

invented a new moulding system especially for this task. Each panel was made up of two sheets of glass, formed in special steel moulds, then laminated together with a sticky PVB interlayer between. The panels were then fixed to the capsules using both silicone sealant and mechanical fixings.

Each capsule has two completely independent electronic operating systems, which are used to turn the capsules and run the air conditioning, helping to prevent condensation and overheating. Each one is also fitted with security cameras, lighting, two-way radio and speakers in the ceiling, while operating systems and back-up batteries are under the floor.

Under certain wind conditions, the top of the rim could sway up to 2–3 metres from side-to-side. Although this would still be safe for the passengers, it would put stress on the metal joints. To eliminate this, 64 mass spring dampers are incorporated onto the rim structure. These reduce the side-to-side sway to a barely perceptible 150mm, making it an exceptionally smooth and comfortable ride.

The capsules were the very last of the wheel's major components to arrive, timed to reach the site when the wheel was already upright. Designed to be just within the maximum width load allowed on French roads, they were wrapped and loaded onto flatbed trailers and driven from Grenoble to Zeebrugge, then shipped to a holding point at Dartford until the wheel was in position. Finally, they were brought by boat up the River Thames and fixed onto the wheel. All 32 capsules were fitted in record time over the course of eight days.

ABOVE The London Eye with its first two passenger capsules fixed into place. All 32 capsules were added to the exterior of the structure over the course of just eight days.

RIGHT The capsules are located on the exterior of the frame, in order to ensure the best possible views of the London landscape. However, standing inside a capsule and looking towards the frame can also provide some dramatic views. Only from inside can you appreciate the intricacy of the structure and its engineering.

design & construction
raising the eye

The huge wheel of the British Airways London Eye – the largest structure ever lifted from horizontal to vertical – was raised in stages. While the architects and engineers had calculated and checked every element of the operation, there was inevitably still some uncertainty attached to the task. Watched by London and the world's media, the team set about fitting the structure with sensors, ready to monitor its movement and progress.

The rim, lying flat over the river, was strapped to the A-frame legs as they lay horizontal above it. The feet of the A-frame were fixed on hinges on the 11 metre high plinths. A second, larger, temporary lifting A-frame was fitted upright to the back of the plinths. Gradually, and with constant monitoring of the sensors in a control room, the wheel was lifted to 35 degrees. Here it was held overnight, sticking precipitously out over the river while the tests and checks were carried out.

The next day, Sunday 10th October 1999, the wheel was lifted to 65 degrees – the final angle of the A-frame legs. It was held at this position, strapped to the legs and projecting dramatically over the river, for a week while the restraining cables, each of which can hold more than 1,100 tonnes, were anchored below Jubilee Gardens. The boarding platform and control rooms were

'The wheel is entirely open and democratic, lighter and airier than any other structure in the land'

Andrew Marr, *The Observer*

also put in place under the wheel. Then, finally, the temporary A-frame was taken down and the wheel untethered from its legs. The wheel could now be slowly rotated from 65 degrees into its final vertical position.

Throughout this period, the eyes of London and the media were on the wheel – especially as this was billed as the second 'lift'. (The first attempt had been dramatically stalled when a safety check showed that a temporary cable was loose.) Yet despite this small setback early on in the procedure, the Eye was successfully raised in full view of its eager audience. The *Evening Standard's* architectural critic, Rowan Moore,

spoke for a whole generation, admitting that his doubts had been wrong, and describing the impromptu 'festival' that took place on the South Bank. Huge crowds gathered on the embankment and the bridges nearby simply to look at the structure.

The new feature had an immediate impact on the city skyline; visible from various parts of London and sitting majestically over the river, it was barely a stone's throw away from another major landmark – the Houses of Parliament. As the capsules gradually arrived and were positioned over the next few days, the wheel slowly established itself as a new landmark for London.

eye view
in context

RIGHT The Royal Festival Hall has been a popular centre for the arts ever since its construction in the 1950s.

BELOW The London Eye sits comfortably on the South Bank, alongside other attractions and landmarks such as the London Aquarium and Jubilee Gardens.

From their very first competition design, Marks Barfield had pinpointed Jubilee Gardens as the ideal site for the London Eye. Here, the great curve of the river puts the Eye right at the centre of London's dispersed, village-based structure, with the City to the north-east and the ancient Palace of Westminster to the south-west. If you draw a circle around the edge of London, the architects say, the London Eye would be right at its centre.

The South Bank is London's great cultural playground. In 1951, the site – till then a muddy river bank – hosted the Festival of Britain and saw the construction of the Royal Festival Hall as well as the temporary celebratory structures, the Skylon Tower and Dome of Discovery. Since then, the area has become one of the world's greatest arts centres, with the addition of the Hayward Gallery, the Queen Elizabeth

Hall, the National Theatre, the National Film Theatre and the bfi London Imax Cinema. The relaxed landscape comprising of river walkways, theatres and cafés was always popular with those who knew the area well.

However, the appeal of the South Bank has rocketed since the turn of the millennium. This interest and enthusiasm is due, in part, to the appearance of the London Eye itself. Together with the reconstructed Shakespeare's Globe Theatre, and the conversion of Bankside Power Station into Tate Modern, the Eye has brought a whole new wave of vibrancy to the area. The converted County Hall building, the riverside walkway and the revitalised interest from both businesses and visitors alike, are all evidence of this growing popularity. Rising above it all, the British Airways London Eye provides a perfect vantage point for observing this new vitality.

1 Former New Scotland Yard   2 Methodist Central Hall   3 Earl's Court   4 Foreign & Commonwealth Office   5 Buckingham Palace   6 Kensington Muse

Downing Street **8** Green Park **9** St James's Park **10** Hyde Park **11** Ministry of Defence **12** RAF Memorial **13** Horse Guards Parade

Nelson's Column, Trafalgar Square **15** National Gallery **16** St Martin-in-the-Fields **17** Whitehall Court

eye view
west

The view to the west exposes London's rural ideals. The home of the reigning monarch (in residence if the Royal Standard flag is flying), Buckingham Palace looks like a country house – which is how it was originally designed. And such country houses, divided vertically, are the model for London's famous West End squares and terraces, built by aristocrats as property developments in the 17th, 18th and 19th centuries. The Royal Parks – St James's in front of Buckingham Palace, Green Park to the right and Hyde Park beyond – were Henry VIII's hunting grounds. The Mall and Pall Mall, leading from the palace to Trafalgar Square, are London's version of 'grand, processional routes' – both designed for games.

Behind Buckingham Palace are the great Victorian museums of Kensington – the Victoria & Albert, the Science Museum and the Natural History Museum. In front of the palace is Whitehall, with its collection of government administrative buildings. Downing Street, the home of the Prime Minister, is clearly visible as the wheel descends. Trafalgar Square, London's only major planned public square, was designed by John Nash, who also created Regent Street and Regent's Park. Nelson's Column in the centre celebrates the great naval victory at Trafalgar. On the western skyline you can see the exhibition buildings of Earl's Court and Trellick Tower, once the tallest housing block in the country.

BOTTOM LEFT The RAF memorial, featuring an eagle, faces the London Eye from the north bank. Behind it lies Whitehall, comprising numerous great architectural features, such as the Banqueting House and Cenotaph.

BELOW Looking from Chelsea Reach, the London Eye rises high above the skyscape. Many familiar structures, such as Westminster Cathedral and Tower 42, sit in apparently close proximity, thanks to the sharp bends of the River Thames.

RIGHT St James's Park was created as one of Henry VIII's hunting parks, and now gives London its green centre. The wheel puts a 'halo' around the buildings of Whitehall.

1 Primrose Hill   2 BT Tower   3 Embankment Place/Charing Cross Station   4 Centrepoint   5 Hampstead Heath   6 British Museum   7 Hungerford Brid

Royal Opera House, Covent Garden   **9** Victoria Embankment   **10** Shell Mex House   **11** Cleopatra's Needle   **12** Alexandra Palace   **13** Somerset House
14 Waterloo Bridge   **15** Royal Courts of Justice and Inns of Court   **16** Royal Festival Hall   **17** Barbican

eye view
north

From the walled Roman city, the wealthy side of London developed gradually west to Soho, the West End and beyond. Marked by the BT Tower and Centrepoint, this area is now considered to be the centre of London, and most of the great traditional institutions are located near here. From the Eye you can see the British Museum, with its great new glass and steel parabolic roof designed by Norman Foster, and the top of the extended Royal Opera House in Covent Garden. The grand palace-style buildings along the river deliberately echo the 16th century string of palaces built along the Thames. For example, Somerset House, beyond Waterloo Bridge, is a building on the site of a 16th century palace. Dating from 1776, it was once the place where births, marriages and deaths were registered, but it now houses the Courtauld Institute of Art. More

recently, Embankment Place, the office development designed by Terry Farrell over Charing Cross station, also adopts this 'river palace' form. Primrose Hill and Hampstead Heath are visible in the distance, as is Alexandra Palace.

RIGHT The sphinxes flanking Cleopatra's Needle on Victoria Embankment are 19th century, but the needle itself is older than London – dating from 1500BC, it was shipped to London in 1877. Its twin is in Central Park, New York. The embankment itself, with its massive water and sewage system beneath, was one of the great infrastructure improvements of the Victorian age.

FAR RIGHT From Primrose Hill, one of the city's projected viewpoints, the London Eye joins the BT Tower in rising above the skyline. The 174 metres tower – 189 metres if you count the mast – was once Britain's tallest structure, and still receives almost all the country's TV programmes through its microwave dishes and switching rooms. The revolving restaurant was closed to the public in 1979 and is now used for charity functions.

1 Inner and Middle Temples 2 Royal Festival Hall 3 Hayward Gallery 4 Royal National Theatre 5 St Paul's Cathedral 6 Oxo Tower 7 Tower 42 (NatWest To

Lloyd's Building   **9** bfi London Imax Cinema   **10** Tate Modern (former Bankside Power Station)   **11** Shell Centre   **12** London Bridge   **13** Tower of London

14 Southwark Cathedral   **15** Tower Bridge   **16** Canary Wharf   **17** Guy's Hospital   **18** Waterloo Station   **19** Greenwich   **20** Waterloo International Station

eye view
east

London has always resisted 'grand plan' developments and its oldest quarter mixes commercial high-rises with buildings a thousand years old. The original Roman walled city of London stretches from the Tower of London (started by William the Conqueror in the 11th century) to St Paul's. The medieval city was destroyed by the Great Fire of 1666 – St Paul's Cathedral and the city churches were rebuilt by Sir Christopher Wren. Wren's plan to rationalise the whole City layout was deemed too expensive and so the modern-day, high-rise city retains its medieval street plan.

Tower 42 (formerly the NatWest Tower and once the tallest building in the UK at 183 metres), was planned in the shape of the bank's three-cornered logo and now hosts the UK's highest bar. The residential towers of the Barbican, with its massive arts centre below, are also prominent. To the right of this, the Lloyd's Building, designed by Richard Rogers, has its lifts, stairs and services exposed on its exterior.

Further east is Canary Wharf, the huge development on London's old docks, with the UK's tallest building at 244 metres. This is now flanked by two other towers almost as high. The Millennium Dome can partly be seen behind. Closer to the Eye, London's old industrial area is being regenerated, led by the transformation of Bankside Power Station into Tate Modern – now the most popular museum of contemporary art in the world. The cultural buildings of the South Bank, the Royal Festival Hall and the National Theatre are at the base of the wheel, with the arched roof of the Eurostar train terminus at Waterloo behind.

BELOW The neon tower of the Hayward Gallery changes colour at different speeds, according to the wind. The gallery, along with the Royal Festival Hall, Queen Elizabeth Hall, Purcell Rooms, National Theatre, National Film Theatre and bfi London IMAX Cinema (near Waterloo Station), helps to make up one of the world's greatest cultural centres.

RIGHT Passengers coming into Waterloo Station can see the London Eye on the final stage of their journey. Visitors arriving via the Eurostar at Waterloo International Station have a tremendous view through the great, asymmetrically curved terminal, which was designed by Nicholas Grimshaw.

BELOW A mix of high-rise and ancient monuments, the city skyline is dominated by St Paul's Cathedral – views of which are carefully protected by law. The Lloyd's Building, designed by Richard Rogers, is one of the world's greatest high-tech buildings with all its services visible on the outside. It was also the first building to use blue feature-lighting – now a popular part of the night-time scene.

1 Crystal Palace   2 The Oval Cricket Ground   3 St Thomas' Hospital   4 County Hall   5 Lambeth Palace   6 Westminster Bridge   7 MI6 Headquarters   8 Lambeth Brid

Vauxhall Bridge   **10** Millbank Tower   **11** Battersea Power Station   **12** Victoria Tower   **13** Houses of Parliament   **14** Department of Transport, Local Government and the Regions

5 Battersea Park   **16** Chelsea Bridge   **17** Big Ben/Clock Tower   **18** St Margaret's, Westminster   **19** Westminster Abbey   **20** Portcullis House

eye view
south

London's ancient structure of scattered riverside developments and villages still survives. Westminster was a royal palace before the Norman Conquest, and William the Conqueror moved his own palace here, to be away from the trading centre of the city. The white stone Westminster Abbey was started in 1245 but was burned down in 1833 when the sticks used to store receipts were privately burned under the Lord's Chamber – an example of 19th century shredding going horribly wrong. Parliament's replacement, which was built over time and that we see today, fuses Victorian technology and fantasy. The Clock Tower, at the base of Westminster Bridge, is more famously known as Big Ben, though this name actually refers to one of the bells inside. Across the river, the Archbishop of Canterbury's palace at Lambeth dates from 1297 and enjoys a leafy seclusion through surrounding trees. County Hall, just below the London Eye, is now home to attractions such as the London Aquarium and the Salvador Dali Museum, as well as a prime location hotel.

Further up the river, you can see the post-modern MI6 building, which featured in the James Bond film 'The World is Not Enough'. It was the first building officially acknowledged as being the home of the UK Secret Service. Moving along, Battersea Power Station, one of the city's most beloved landmarks, though derelict since the 1980s, is visible. And further across the horizon, the Crystal Palace TV mast marks the outer edge of London.

LEFT The curved façade of the Edwardian County Hall was originally designed to face the other way. Built as a home to the London County Council, which then became the Labour-controlled GLC, the building was eventually sold off in the 1980s.

BELOW LEFT Looking down the river from Vauxhall, the London Eye can clearly be seen projecting out over the embankment.

BELOW The design of the Palace of Westminster, a familiar London icon, was actually the result of fierce, Victorian classical-gothic 'style wars'. Designed by the staunch classicist Charles Barry, the building was 'decorated' by the gothic architect Pugin. 'Tudor details on a classic body,' Barry called it. The building is still one of the most popular of London's landmarks.

eye view
from above

1 Victoria & Albert Museum   2 The Serpentine   3 Harrods   4 Hyde Park   5 Marble Arch   6 Hyde Park Corner   7 Oxford Street   8 Green Park   9 Oxford Circ

18 Horse Guards Parade   19 Whitehall   20 Houses of Parliament   21 Covent Garden   22 Hungerford Bridge   23 BA London Eye (under constructi

31 Waterloo International Station   32 Waterloo Station   33 Imperial War Museum   34 Blackfriars Bridge   35 St Paul's Cathedral   36 Millennium Bridge   37 Tate Mode

Buckingham Palace   **11** Regent Street   **12** The Mall   **13** Piccadilly Circus   **14** St James's Park   **15** Leicester Square   **16** National Gallery   **17** Trafalgar Square

Westminster Bridge   **25** Lambeth Bridge   **26** County Hall   **27** Aldwych   **28** Waterloo Bridge   **29** Royal National Theatre   **30** Royal Festival Hall

Globe Theatre   **39** Southwark Bridge   **40** London Bridge   **41** HMS Belfast   **42** Greater London Authority   **43** Tower of London   **44** Tower Bridge

eye
facts & figures

Height of London Eye: 135 metres. It is the tallest observation wheel in the world; three-quarters of the height of the BT Tower and four-sevenths of the height of Canary Wharf. When built, it was the fourth tallest structure in London.

Weight of London Eye: 2,100 tonnes.

Number of capsules: 32. Originally 60 capsules were planned, but the design was later modified.

Length of flight: Approximately half an hour.

Speed: 0.26 metres per second, a quarter of the average walking speed.

Number of people carried at any one time: 800. This equates to 25 people per capsule.

Viewing distance: Up to 40 kilometres.

Spindle: 25 metres long, including the 10 metre-long hub that passes over the spindle. The spindle has a diameter of 2.1 metres, (the hub is 4.5 metres in diameter). The spindle was cast in eight sections – the largest section was more than 5 metres long and required 160 tonnes of molten steel.

A-frame legs: 58 metres long – three-fifths the height of Big Ben. They stand 20 metres apart on cast bases,

weighing about 23 tonnes each. The whole A-frame weighs 310 tonnes.

Wheel cables: 16 rim rotation cables, each around 60mm thick. In addition, there are 64 spoke cables, which are all 70mm thick and are spun of 121 individual strands in layers. At this scale, a bicycle wheel's spokes would be 0.33mm thick.

Backstay cables: There are four in total, each 110mm in diameter. They weigh 19 tonnes.

Foundations: The compression foundation under the legs required 2,200 tonnes of concrete and 45 concrete piles – each being 33 metres deep. The tension foundation, holding the backstay cables, used 1,200 tonnes of concrete.

Glass: 13.2mm thick, laminated and fixed using silicone.

Weight of rotating wheel structure: 1,200 tonnes.

Weight of rim: 800 tonnes. The rim includes 64 'dampers', each with a mass of 500kg and adjusted to cope with wind; without this the wheel would sway sideways 2–3 metres. The sway is 150mm with dampers.

Weight of capsules: Each capsule weighs 11 tonnes.

Weight of hub and spindle: 335 tonnes.

Number of people employed in construction: 2,000 including an entire alpine village who assisted in testing the capsule embarkation procedures.

Time taken to build: Less than 16 months from start of fabrication of components to operation.

Total cost of the project: £75 million.

eye
awards

Since opening in 2000, the British Airways London Eye has won numerous awards for both tourism and architecture.

- MBE – presented to David Marks and Julia Barfield in 2000
- Pride of Britain Awards – in recognition of ordinary people making exceptional achievements
- British Incoming Tour Operators Association – Visitor attraction of the year 2000
- London Tourism Awards 2000 – The peoples choice award
- Architectural Practice of the Year, 2001 – For entrepreneurial spirit, vision and commitment
- Corus Construction Award, 2000 – To recognise high standards of architectural and structural design for outstanding structures built in the UK and the Netherlands in the run up to the millennium
- Best British Innovation Award, 2001
- Travellers Choice Awards 2001 – Best millennium attraction
- Tourism for Tomorrow Award – Highly commended in the built environment category
- London First Millennium Awards – Outstanding contribution to architecture
- Walpole Award, 2001 – Best British innovation

- D & AD Awards, 2001 – Gold and silver award for the most outstanding environmental design and architecture
- Design Week Special Award, 2001 – Honouring creative excellence in design
- Royal Institute of British Architects Award for Architecture – Recognising excellence, technical consistency and fitness for purpose in architecture
- American Institute of Architects (London UK chapter) Design Award Overall Winner (awarded jointly) – Recognising design excellence for a built project
- Dupont Benedictus Awards for Innovation – Special merit
- Prince Philip Designers Prize – Presented to David Marks and Julia Barfield for outstanding lifetime achievement in design for business and society
- Royal Institute of Chartered Surveyors – Winner of special award given in recognition of excellence
- The Institute of Structural Engineers – Special structural award
- National Steel Awards 2000, Netherlands
- Blueprint Award – Best new public building
- Leisure Property Forum Awards – Best national scheme, best regeneration scheme and best innovative concept
- European Award for Steel Structures, 2001 – Overall winner throughout europe for outstanding design and construction

eye
booking details

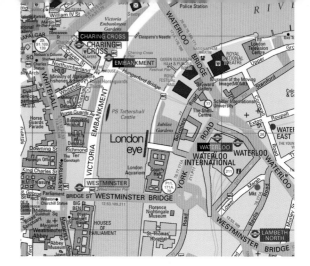

How to book a flight

British Airways London Eye operates a system of timed flights.
You will be able to book a date and time for your flight in advance.
The flight itself takes half an hour. You will need to arrive at the
attraction 30 minutes prior to your flight time in order to allow time
to collect your tickets and to board the Eye.

1 Book on-line at **www.ba-londoneye.com**
On this internet booking service you will be able to book a flight
for a maximum of 24 guests or book a private capsule.
2 Call **+44 (0)870 5000 600** (24 hour service)
On this automated booking line, you will be able to book a flight
for a maximum of 24 guests.
3 Buy On-site
You can visit the Ticket Hall within County Hall for both advance
and same day tickets.

Groups of 25 or more customers

For groups of 25 or more, please call **+44 (0)870 990 8886**
(8.30am to 6.30pm daily).

Disabled bookings

Disabled guests receive a special discount and service if they book on
our disabled booking line on **+44 (0)870 990 8885** (8.30am to 6.30pm
daily). For safety reasons, there is a limit to the number of wheelchairs
allowed on the flight at one time. Therefore, wheelchair users are
advised to book in advance on this line.

Private capsule hire

Up to 25 guests may enjoy their own private capsule and a personal fast
track on to the Eye. You can have hospitality such as champagne
served in your capsule. Please call **+44 (0)870 220 2223** or email:
capsules@ba-londoneye.com.

General information

Nearest Stations: Waterloo tube and mainline and Westminster tube
station (both 5 minutes away).

To contact us please write to Customer Services,
British Airways London Eye, Riverside Building,
County Hall, Westminster Bridge Road SE1 7PB.
Tel: +44 (0)870 990 8883 **Fax:** +44 (0)870 990 8884
Email: customer.services@ba-londoneye.com

First published in 2002 by HarperCollins*Publishers*, 77–85 Fulham Palace Road,
London, W6 8JB. The HarperCollins website address is: www.**fire**and**water**.com

Text © HarperCollins*Publishers*

Photography © Nick Wood except page 8 © Sophie Jones, page 9 illustration
© Marks Barfield Associates, page 11 © Ian Lambot, pages 16 &17 illustrations
© Nic Bailey, page 18 © Lisa Young, page 25 © Royal Festival Hall – photo by
Richard Haughton, page 42/43 © Get Mapping plc, page 46 left © Sam Scott-
London Eye, page 48 Mapping © Bartholomew Ltd 2001

Written by Kester Rattenbury
Design: Clare Baggaley
Editorial: Angela Newton

The publishers have made every effort to ensure that the information contained in
this book is accurate and as up-to-date as possible at the time of publication.

ISBN 0 00 764267 9

Colour reproduction by Colourscan. Printed and bound in Italy

The official imaging partner of British Airways London Eye

Coca-Cola Enterprises Ltd
The official soft drink partner of
British Airways London Eye

Nestlé
The official confectionery partner
of British Airways London Eye

Nikon
The official binoculars partner of
British Airways London Eye

STORM
The official timing partner of
British Airways London Eye